PRESENTED TO

....

FROM

....

DATE

....

DADS & SONS

*Timeless wisdom
and reflections on teaching,
guiding, and loving your son—
his whole life long*

DR. JAMES DOBSON

TYNDALE
MOMENTUM

*An Imprint of
Tyndale House Publishers, Inc.*

Visit Tyndale online at www.tyndale.com.

TYNDALE is a registered trademark of Tyndale House Publishers, Inc. *Tyndale Momentum* and the Tyndale Momentum logo are trademarks of Tyndale House Publishers, Inc. Tyndale Momentum is an imprint of Tyndale House Publishers, Inc.

Dads and Sons

Literary development and design: Koechel Peterson & Associates, Inc., Minneapolis, Minnesota.

This book has been adapted from *Bringing Up Boys: Practical Advice and Encouragement for Those Shaping the Next Generation of Men*, copyright © 2001 by James C. Dobson. Published by Tyndale House Publishers.

Printed in China

20 19 18 17 16 15 14
7   6   5   4   3   2   1

CONTENTS

The Wonderful
World of Boys

Greetings to all the men out there who are blessed to be called dads. There is no greater privilege in living than bringing a tiny new human being into the world and then trying to raise him or her properly during the next eighteen years. Doing that job right requires all the intelligence, wisdom, and determination you will be able to muster from day to day. And for fathers whose family includes one or more boys, the greatest challenge may be just keeping them alive through childhood and adolescence.

In case you haven't noticed, boys are different from girls. That fact was never in question for previous generations. They knew intuitively that each sex was a breed apart and that boys were typically the more unpredictable of the two. Haven't you heard your parents and grandparents say with a smile, "Girls are made out of sugar and spice and everything nice, but boys are made of snakes and snails and puppy-dog tails"? It was said tongue-in-cheek, but people of all ages thought it was based on fact. "Boys will be boys," they said knowingly. They were right.

Boys are usually (but not always) tougher to raise than their sisters are. Girls can be difficult to handle too, but there is something especially challenging about boys. Although individual temperaments vary, boys are designed to be more assertive, audacious, and excitable than girls are. Psychologist John Rosemond calls them "little aggressive machines."[1]

> *One father referred to his son as "all afterburner and no rudder."*

Not unlike other boys, our son, Ryan, encountered one dangerous situation after another as a boy. By the time he was six, he was personally acquainted with many of the local emergency room attendants and doctors. And why not? He had been their patient repeatedly. One day when he was about four, he was running through the backyard with his eyes closed and fell into a decorative metal "plant." One of the steel rods stuck him in the right eyebrow and exposed the bone underneath. He came staggering through the back door bathed in blood, a memory that still gives Shirley nightmares. Off they went to the trauma center—*again!*

What makes young males act like that? What inner force compels them to teeter on the edge of disaster? What is it about the masculine temperament that drives boys to tempt the laws of gravity and ignore the gentle voice of common sense—the one that says, "Don't do it, Son"?

Boys are like this because of the way they are wired neurologically and because of the influence of hormones that stimulate certain aggressive behavior. You can't understand males of any age, including yourself, without knowing something about the forces that operate within.

We want to help you raise "good" boys in this postmodern age. The culture is at war with the family, especially its youngest

and most vulnerable members. Harmful and enticing messages are shouted at them from movies and television, from the rock-music industry, from the advocates of so-called safe-sex ideology, from homosexual activists, and from the readily available obscenity and pornography on the Internet. The question confronting parents is, "How can we steer our boys and girls past the many negative influences that confront them on every side?" It is an issue with eternal implications.

Our purpose in this regard will be to assist you as you "play defense" on behalf of your sons—that is, as you protect boys from immoral and dangerous enticements. But that is not enough. You also need to "play offense"—to capitalize on the impressionable years of childhood by instilling in your sons the antecedents of character. Your assignment during two brief decades will be to transform your boys from immature and flighty youngsters into honest, caring men who will be respectful of women, loyal and faithful in marriage, keepers of commitments, strong and decisive leaders, good workers, and secure in their masculinity. And of course, the ultimate goal for people of faith is to give each child an understanding of Scripture and a lifelong passion for Jesus Christ. This is, I believe, the most important responsibility for those of us who have been entrusted with the care and nurturance of children.

So buckle your seat belt.
We have a lot of interesting
ground to cover.

This Is
What Boys Do

*In an article entitled, "What Are Boys Made Of?"
reporter Paula Gray Hunker quoted a mother named
Meg MacKenzie who said raising her two sons is like
living with a tornado. "From the moment that they come
home from school, they'll be running around the house,
climbing trees outside and making a commotion inside
that sounds as if a herd of elephants has moved in
upstairs. I'll try to calm them down, but my husband will
say, 'This is what boys do. Get used to it.'"* [2]

I was one of those boys who lived on the edge of disaster. When I was about ten, I was very impressed by the way Tarzan could swing through the trees from vine to vine. No one ever told me, "Don't try this at home." I climbed high into a pear tree one day and tied a rope to a small limb. Then I positioned myself for a journey to the next tree. Unfortunately, I made a small but highly significant miscalculation. The rope was longer than the distance from the limb to the ground. I kept thinking all the way down that something didn't seem right. I was still gripping the rope when I landed flat on my back twelve feet below and knocked all the air out of the state of Oklahoma. I couldn't breathe for what seemed like an hour (it must have been about ten seconds) and was sure I was dying. Two teeth were broken and a loud gonging sound echoed in my head. But later that afternoon, I was up and running again. No big deal. The next year I blew the most beautiful blue stuff all over the ceiling of my room with my chemistry set.

Does my behavior sound familiar? If you host a birthday party for five-year-olds, the boys will probably throw cake, put their hands in the punch bowl, or mess up the games for the girls. Why are they like this? Some would say their mischievous nature has been learned from the culture. Really? Then why are boys more aggressive in every society around the globe? And why did the Greek philosopher Plato write more than 2,300 years ago,

"Of all the animals, the boy is the most unmanageable"? [3]

One of the scariest aspects of raising boys is their tendency to risk life and limb for no good reason. It begins very early. If a toddler can climb on it, he will jump off it. He careens out of control toward tables, tubs, pools, steps, trees, and streets. He makes "guns" out of cucumbers or toothbrushes and likes digging around in drawers, pill bottles, and Mom's purse. And just hope he doesn't get his grubby little hands on a tube of lipstick.

A boy harasses grumpy dogs and picks up kitties by their ears. He loves to throw rocks, play with fire, and shatter glass. He also gets great pleasure out of irritating his brothers and sisters, his mother, his teachers, and other children. As he gets older, he is drawn to everything dangerous—skateboards, rock climbing, hang gliding, motorcycles, and mountain bikes. At about sixteen, he and his buddies begin driving around town like kamikaze pilots on sake. It's a wonder any of them survive. Not every boy is like this, of course, but the majority of them are.

A study by Canadian psychologist Barbara Morrongiello showed that females tend to think hard about whether or not they could get hurt, and they are less likely to plunge ahead if there is any potential for injury. Boys, however, will take a chance if they think the danger is worth the risk. Impressing their friends (and eventually girls) is usually considered worth the risk. A related study by Licette Peterson confirmed that girls are more fearful than boys are. For example, they brake sooner when riding their bikes. They react more negatively to pain and try not to make the same mistake twice. Boys, on the other hand, are slower to learn from calamities. They tend to think that their injuries were caused by "bad luck."[4] Maybe their luck will be better next time.

Besides, scars are cool.

Why do boys tend to be competitive, aggressive, and assertive?

The answers can be found . . .

So What Is the Difference?

The impact of testosterone will have many profound influences on a boy's developing mind and body. In fact, it will affect his every thought and deed for the rest of his life.

So what makes young males act as they do? Why do boys tend to be competitive, aggressive, assertive, and lovers of cars, trucks, guns, and balls? The answers can be found in three physical features and processes—hormones, serotonin, and the amygdala—that operate from within, which are very important to our understanding of boys.

The first factor to be considered is the hormone testosterone, which is largely responsible for maleness. It shows up at six or seven weeks after conception, when all embryos are technically "female."[5] That is when a dramatic spiking of testosterone occurs for those who have inherited a "Y" (or male) chromosome. It begins masculinizing their tiny bodies and transforming them into boys. In a real sense, this "hormonal bath," as it is sometimes called, actually damages the walnut-shaped brain and alters its structure in many ways. Even its color changes. The corpus callosum, which is the rope of nerve fibers that connects the two hemispheres, is made less efficient. That limits the number of electrical transmissions that can flow from one side of the brain to the other, which will have lifelong implications. Later, a man will have to think longer about what he believes, especially about something with an emotional component. He may never fully comprehend it.

A woman, on the other hand, will typically be able to access her prior experience from both hemispheres and discern almost instantly how she feels about it.

Another consequence of this flood of testosterone in the prenatal period is the localization of language development. For a right-handed man, it is isolated largely in the left hemisphere of his brain. For a woman, it is better distributed on both sides. For this reason, she will probably be more articulate than he from early childhood. Life just isn't fair.

Another flood of testosterone will occur at the beginning of puberty, which will transform him from a boy to a man. (After puberty, testosterone in males is twenty times that in females,[6] and estrogen in females is twenty times that in males.[7]) It is this second hormonal burst that is primarily responsible for the sudden appearance of facial and pubic hair, squeaky voices, pimply faces, larger muscles, sexual awakening, and, eventually, other characteristics of adult masculinity.

This powerful substance accounts for at least some of the strange behavior that drives parents crazy. It explains why a happy, cooperative twelve-year-old boy can suddenly turn into a sullen, depressed adolescent at thirteen. Human chemistry appears to go haywire for a time. There's a tendency for parents to despair during this period because everything they've tried to teach seems to have misfired. Self-discipline, cleanliness, respect for authority, the work ethic, and even common courtesy may look like lost causes for several years. But better days are coming. The mechanisms that set kids aflame will eventually cool down. That's why I recommend that you not look too quickly for the person your child will become and seek to "just get them through it" rather than try to fix everything that bugs you.

The masculine engine continues to be fueled by testosterone throughout life. For sake of space, I must summarize the research, but testosterone is clearly correlated with psychological and interpersonal and social dominance, confident physicality, high self-esteem, and in particular drives the masculine interest in sports and outdoor activities. Men, in whose bodies surge ten to twenty times as much testosterone as in women, are more likely to reach for wealth, power, fame, and status because they are urged in that direction from within. Women are more interested in relationships than in coming out on top.

> *Most experts believe boys' tendency to take risks, to be more assertive, to fight and compete, to argue, to boast, and to excel at certain skills, such as problem solving, math, and science, is directly linked to the way the brain is hardwired and to the presence of testosterone. This may explain why boys have "ants in their pants" when they are in the classroom and why teachers call them little "wiggly worms." The problem is that boys are often taught at such a tempo that it becomes difficult for them to adjust.*

Testosterone also accounts for boys' early desire to be the strongest, bravest, toughest, rootin-shootin hombré on the range.

It's just the way God made boys.

So What
Is the Difference?
(Part 2)

If testosterone is the gasoline that powers the male brain, the hormone serotonin slows the speed and helps one steer. Serotonin carries information from one nerve cell to another, and its purpose is to pacify or soothe the emotions and to help an individual control his or her impulsive behavior. It also facilitates good judgment.

And . . . you guessed it.
Females typically have more of it than males.

The third aspect of neurobiology that helps us understand the differences between males and females concerns a portion of the brain known as the amygdala, which functions as a small but powerful "emotional computer." When a physical or emotional threat is perceived by the senses, the amygdala instantly orders the adrenal glands and other defensive organs to release various hormones that maximize the chances for survival during times of imminent danger.

What makes the amygdala of interest to us is its role in regulating aggression. It sits smack-dab in the middle of the hypothalamus at the base of the brain, which is the seat of the emotions. When the amygdala perceives a threat or challenge, it fires electrical impulses by way of neural connections into the hypothalamus that put it in a nasty mood. Add testosterone to that situation and you have the potential for a fiery response. Let me emphasize this final point: the amygdala can respond only to what is in its memory bank. It does not think or reason. It emits an "irrational" chemical and electrical response that may save your life in an emergency—but it can also precipitate violence and make matters much worse.[8]

Well, here we go again. The amygdala is larger in males than in females, which helps explain why boys are more likely than girls to be volatile and to engage in what psychotherapist Michael Gurian called "morally-at-risk behavior." [9]

Together, these three critical components of male neurophysiology—testosterone, serotonin, and the amygdala—determine what it means to be masculine and why boys are a "breed apart." Having considered what might be viewed as the downside of these features, I must hasten to say that boys and men have their share of neurological advantages, too. Because of the specialization of their brains, males are typically better than females at math, science, spatial relations, logic, and reasoning. This is why most architects, mathematicians, and physical scientists are men. It is also interesting that males are more responsive to stories than women. When they get together, they share experiences that convey emotional meaning for them, whereas women almost never do this. Women talk more openly about their feelings rather than playing the game called "Can you top this?" In short, the sexes are very, very different in ways that may never be fully understood.

How incredibly creative it is of God to put a different form of dominance in each sex so that there is a balance between the two. When they come together in marriage to form what Scripture calls "one flesh," they complement and supplement one another (Matthew 19:4-5). This is the divine plan. It leaves no doubt that the Creator made not one sex but two, each beautifully crafted to "fit with" and meet the needs of the other.

That brings us back to our understanding of boys. Remember that they are men-in-training. Their aggressive nature is designed for a purpose. It prepares them for the "provision and protection" roles to come. That assertiveness also builds culture when properly channeled. I urge you as parents not to resent or try to eliminate the aggressive and excitable nature that can be so irritating. That temperament is part of a divine plan.

Celebrate it. Enjoy it.
Thank God for it.

But also understand that it needs to be
shaped, molded, and "civilized."

Remember that
they are men-in-training.

Celebrate your son's temperament. Enjoy it. Thank God for it.

Preserving
Your Son's Spirit

Now, more than ever, boys are experiencing a
crisis of confidence that reaches deep within the
soul. Many of them are growing up believing
they are unloved by their parents and are hated
or disrespected by their peers.

It is our job as adults to see that each of our children finds the security he or she needs. That includes the vulnerability your son feels to his peers, which has always been part of the human experience, but today's children and teens are even more sensitive to it. The reason is that popular culture has become a tyrannical master that demands ever-greater conformity to its shifting ideal of perfection.

For instance, in our culture little boys want desperately to be big, powerful, and handsome. By the age of four, they will flex their little biceps by holding up their arms, making a fist, and pointing to the bump where a muscle will someday grow (hopefully). Young boys wear Superman and Batman capes, cowboy clothes, and the funny little loincloths Tarzan wore.

This masculine "will to power"
is why boys fight, climb, wrestle, strut, and show off.
It is the way they are made.

This is why when a boy is slow in developing or is smaller than his peers, he often suffers from self-image problems. Just put yourself in the position of a tiny boy who is taunted and shoved around by every other kid in his class and who lacks the strength to compete in sports—the one who is called "Runt" or "Squirt." After he runs that gauntlet for a few years, his spirit begins to bleed.

Most of us have been taunted or ridiculed by our peers. But we must never underestimate the distress that can occur in what looks like "no big deal" to us, especially for kids who are already wounded from other sources. We must never forget the difficulties of trying to grow up in the competitive world in which a child lives.

*Take a moment to listen,
to care, and to direct such a youngster.
That may be the best investment of your life.*

To preserve the spirit of your son may require extraordinary and inconvenient measures. I would not permit my child to stay in an abusive environment if I perceived it as more than the usual bickering between kids. If peers begin to gang up on your son and are ripping into his heart day after day, get him out of there. I would find a magnet school, or a Christian school, or a way to homeschool, or I would even move to another city if necessary. Whatever the approach taken, you must protect the spirit of your child. I have seen firsthand what a pack of wolves can do to a defenseless lamb.

Here's the tricky part. While you are working behind the scenes to protect your child from abuse, you must not make him feel victimized beyond the immediate circumstance. It is very easy to give a boy the idea that the world is out to get him. That overarching sense of victimization paralyzes a person and makes him throw up his hands in despair. Once he yields to the insidious notion that he can't win—that he is set up for failure—he becomes demoralized. The will to overcome adversity is weakened. Talk to your boys not about the wider world that is stacked against them, but teach them how to deal with the isolated situation that has arisen. I hope this is clear.

> *You must never make your child think you*
> *believe he is destined for failure and rejection.*
> *He will believe you!*

*It is our job as adults to see that
each of our children finds the
security he or she needs.*

The Essential Father

*Boys are constructed emotionally
to be dependent on dads in ways that were
not understood until recently.*

Chief among the threats to this generation of boys is the breakdown of the family. Every other difficulty we will consider has been caused by or is related to that fundamental tragedy. It can hardly be overstated. We have been emphasizing for years that stable, lifelong marriages provide the foundation for social order. Everything of value rests on those underpinnings. In cultures where divorce becomes commonplace or large numbers of men and women choose to live together or copulate without bothering to marry, untold millions of kids are caught in the chaos and suffer the most from it.

Nations that are populated largely by immature, immoral, weak-willed, cowardly, and self-indulgent men cannot and will not long endure. These types of men include those who sire and abandon their children; who cheat on their wives; who lie, steal, and covet; who hate their countrymen; and who serve no god but money. That is the direction culture is taking today's boys.

We must make the necessary investment to counter these influences and to build within our boys lasting qualities of character, self-discipline, respect for authority, commitment to the truth, a belief in the work ethic, and an unshakable love for Jesus Christ.

A father holds awesome power in the lives of his children, for good or ill. Families have understood that fact for centuries. When asked who their heroes are, the majority of boys who are fortunate enough to have a father will say, "It's my dad." On the other hand, when a father is uninvolved—when he doesn't love or care for his kids—it creates an ache, a longing, that will linger for decades.

We now know that there are two critical periods during childhood when boys are particularly vulnerable. The most obvious occurs at the onset of puberty, when members of both sexes experience an emotional and hormonal upheaval and desperately need their father's supervision, guidance, and love. Divorce at that time, more than at others, is typically devastating to boys.

But according to Dr. Carol Gilligan, professor at Harvard University, there is another critical period earlier in life—one not shared by girls. Very young boys bask in their mother's femininity and womanliness during infancy and toddlerhood. Fathers are important then, but mothers are primary. At about three to five years of age, however, a lad gradually pulls away from his mom and sisters in an effort to formulate a masculine identity.[10] It is typical for boys during those years, and even earlier, to crave the attention and involvement of their dad and to try to emulate his behavior and mannerisms.

I remember my son clearly identifying with my masculinity when he was in that period between kindergarten and first grade. For example, as our family prepared to leave in the car, Ryan would say, "Hey, Dad. Us guys will get in the front seat and the girls will sit in the back." He wanted it known that he was a "guy" just like me. I was keenly aware that he was patterning his behavior and masculinity after mine. That's the way the system is supposed to work.

But when fathers are absent, inaccessible, distant, or abusive at that time, their boys have only a vague notion of what it means to be male. One of the primary objectives of parents is to help boys identify their gender assignments and understand what it means to be a man.

> *My point is: While you're climbing the*
> *ladder of success, don't forget your own*
> *family. Those years with your children at*
> *home will be gone in a heartbeat. And do*
> *not squander today's opportunities to relate*
> *to your son or to teach him what it means to*
> *be a man. Do whatever is necessary to grab*
> *those precious moments, whether it requires*

changing jobs, getting a smaller house,
or turning down lucrative and exciting
opportunities. Nothing is worth losing your
kids. Nothing!

Understanding Boys and Girls

Don't you love the spontaneity and creativity of children? Boys and girls have such a fresh take on almost everything, and as we have seen, they view life from opposite ends of the universe. Even a child can see that boys and girls are different. Unfortunately, what is obvious to most children and adults became the object of heated controversy in the 1970s, when a goofy new idea took root. A small but noisy band of feminists began insisting that the sexes were identical except for their reproductive apparatus, and that any uniqueness in temperament or behavior resulted from patriarchal cultural biases.[11]

It was a radical concept that lacked any scientific support, except that which was flawed and politically motivated. Nevertheless, the campaign penetrated the entire culture. Suddenly, professors and professionals who should have known better began nodding in agreement. No doubt about it. Males and females were redundant. Parents had been wrong about their kids for at least five thousand years. The media ran with the notion and the word *unisex* found its way into the language of the enlightened. Anyone who challenged the new dogma, as I did in a 1975 book titled *What Wives Wish Their Husbands Knew about Women,* was branded as sexist or something worse.

The feminist movement then took a new and dangerous turn. Its leaders began trying to redesign the way children were being raised (which is why the issue is of concern to us today, all these years later). Television talk-show host Phil Donahue and dozens of wannabes told parents day after day that their daughters were victims of terrible sexist bias and that their sons should be raised more like girls. There was great urgency to their message.

Things had to change immediately! they said.

Donahue's feminist girlfriend and later wife, Marlo Thomas, coauthored a bestselling book at about the same time titled *Free to Be You and Me,* which the publishers described as "the first real guide to nonsexist child rearing." It urged boys to play with dolls and tea sets and told them they could be anything they wanted to be, including (no kidding!) "grandmas and mommies." It featured dozens of poems and stories about role reversals, such as a mother nailing shingles on the roof, building new shelves in the family room, and working with cement. Meanwhile, Father was in the kitchen making breakfast. Every effort was made to teach kids that fathers made great moms and mothers were pretty tough dudes.[12] The book sold several million copies. And the movement had only just begun.

Germaine Greer, author of *The Female Eunuch,* was even more extreme. She said the traditional family had "castrated women." She believed mothers should be less nurturing of their daughters because to treat them gently and kindly would reinforce sexual stereotypes and make them more "dependent" and feminine. Greer also insisted that children are better off being raised by institutions rather than parents.[13] It is difficult to believe today that her book offering those and similarly outrageous views also soared to the top of all the bestseller lists. That illustrates just how culturally dominant radical feminism was at that time.

Perhaps the most influential of the early feminists was Gloria Steinem, founder of the National Organization for Women and editor of *Ms.* magazine. Here is a sampling of her perspective on marriage and child rearing:

> *We've had a lot of people in this country who have had the courage to raise their daughters more like their sons. Which is great because it means they're more equal. . . . But there are many fewer people who have had the courage to raise their sons more like their daughters. And that's what needs to be done.*[14]
>
> *We need to stop raising boys to think that they need to prove their masculinity by being controlling or by not showing emotion or by not being little girls. You can ask [boys] . . . "What if you were a little girl?" They get very upset at the very idea they might be this inferior thing. They've already got this*

idea that in order to be boys they have to be
superior to girls and that's the problem.[15]

[Marriage is] not an equal partnership.
I mean, you lose your name, your credit
rating, your legal residence, and socially,
you're treated as if his identity were yours. I
can't imagine being married. If everybody
has to get married, then clearly it is a prison,
not a choice.[16] *(Steinem married in 2000.)*

All women are supposed to want
children. But I could never drum up any
feelings of regret.[17]

Think for a moment about the above quotes from Steinem, Greer, and the other early feminists. Most of them were never married, didn't like children, and deeply resented men, yet they advised millions of women about how to raise their children and, especially, how to produce healthy boys. There is no evidence that Steinem or Greer ever had any significant experience with children of either sex. Isn't it interesting that the media (to my knowledge) never homed in on that incongruity? And isn't it sad that these women were allowed to twist and warp the attitudes of a generation of kids?

Of major concern to the feminists was what they considered to be the "sexism" in children's toys. As with so many issues during that era, it was Germaine Greer who was most vocal. She said, "So where does the difference [between the sexes] come from? If it's all bred into us by people like toy makers, who steer boys toward these trucks, girls to the dolls, and by teachers, parents, employers—all the wicked influences of a sexist society—then maybe this is a social problem that needs to be fixed."[18]

Great pressure was exerted on companies to "fix" the problem.

Christina Hoff Sommers addressed the flap over toys in her outstanding book, *The War against Boys.* She reported that Hasbro Toys tried to accommodate feminists by producing a new dollhouse designed to interest both boys and girls. That way they could sell twice as many units. There was, however, a slight miscalculation in the way children would respond. Girls tended to "play house," using the plastic structure in the traditional way. Their dolls got married, arranged toy furniture, had babies, and did the things they had seen their mothers doing. The boys played with the dollhouse too, but not as anticipated. They catapulted the baby carriage off the roof and generally messed up the game for the girls.[19]

Back to the drawing board.

Clearly, there are serious implications here for mothers and fathers. I urge you to protect your boys from those who are espousing these postmodern views. Shield both your sons and daughters from gender feminism and from those who would seek to confuse their sexuality. Protect the masculinity of your boys, who will be under increasing political pressure in years to come. Buffer them from the perception that most adult males are sexual predators who are violent and disrespectful to women.

It is also important for us as adults to understand our own sexual identities. If we don't know who we are, our kids will be doubly confused about who they are. Any

uncertainty, any ambiguity in that assignment must be seen as damaging not only to our sons and daughters but also to the long-term stability of society itself.

> *Finally, I urge you to base your teachings*
> *about sexuality on the Scriptures, which tell*
> *us, "God created man in his own image,*
> *in the image of God he created him; male*
> *and female he created them" (Genesis 1:27).*
> *Jesus, who was the first Jewish leader to give*
> *dignity and status to women, said, "Haven't*
> *you read . . . that at the beginning the*
> *Creator 'made them male and female,'" and,*
> *"For this reason a man will leave his father*
> *and mother and be united to his wife, and*
> *the two will become one flesh" (Matthew*
> *19:4-5). That is the divine plan. It leaves no*
> *doubt that the Creator made not one sex but*
> *two, each beautifully crafted to "fit with"*
> *and meet the needs of the other. Any effort*
> *to teach children differently is certain to*
> *produce turmoil in the soul of a child.*

Protect the masculinity
of your boys.

Make Warm Memories

I only wanted to know that Dad was there!

I was blessed to have a wonderful father who was accessible to me from the earliest years of childhood. I'm told that when I was two years of age, my family lived in a one-bedroom apartment, and my little bed was located beside that of my parents. My father said later that it was very common during that time for him to awaken at night to a little voice that was whispering, "Daddy? Daddy?" My father would answer quietly, "What, Jimmy?" And I would say, "Hold my hand!" Dad would reach across the darkness and grope for my little hand, finally just engulfing it in his own. He said the instant he had my hand firmly in his grip, my arm would become limp and my breathing deep and regular. I'd immediately gone back to sleep. You see, I only wanted to know that he was there!

I have a catalog of warm memories of my dad from the preschool years. One day when I was nearly three, I was at home with my mother and heard a knock on the front door.

"Go see who it is," she said with a little smile on her face.

I opened the door and there stood my dad. He took my hand and said, "Come with me. I want to show you something." He led me to the side of the house, where he had hidden a big blue tricycle. It was one of the wonderful moments of my life. On another day during that same year, I recall trotting beside my big dad (he was six foot four) and feeling very proud to be with him. I even recall how huge his hand felt as it held mine.

I also remember the delightful times I roughhoused with my father. Many moms fail to understand why that kind of foolishness is important, but it is. Just as wolf cubs and leopard kittens romp and fight with each other, boys of all ages love to rumble. When I was five years old, my dad and I used to horrify my mother by having all-out kick fights. That's right! Kick fights! He weighed 180 pounds and I tipped the scales at about 50, but we went at each other like sumo wrestlers. He would entice me to kick his shins and then, inevitably, he would block my thrust with the bottom of his foot. That made me go after him again with a vengeance. Then dad would tap me on the shin with his toe. Believe it or not, this was wonderful fun for me. We would end up laughing hysterically, despite the bumps and bruises on my legs. My mother would demand that we stop, having no clue about why I loved this game. It was just a guy thing.

Some might say that this "violence" at home could lead to criminal behavior. Likewise, many have concluded that corporal punishment, even when administered in a loving environment, teaches kids to hurt others. They are wrong. It isn't roughhousing or measured discipline that predisposes boys to misbehavior. It is often the absence of a father who can teach them how to be men and correct them authoritatively when they are wrong.

It's just a guy thing.

Fathers and Sons

Despite all the challenges associated with raising a rambunctious son, one of the greatest privileges in living is to have him hug your neck and say, "I love you, Dad."

Boys have a way of frustrating and irritating the very souls of us dads. They leave our best tools out in the rain, lose our binoculars, and drop our cameras. Many of them are sassy, irresponsible, hard to handle, and do things that make absolutely no sense to the rational mind. Of course, we were boys once who drove our own dads crazy, so we should cut our sons some slack.

Let's look a little more closely at what it means to be a father of boys. I want to focus on the two primary ways a dad's influence is transmitted at home, beginning with modeling. If character training is a primary goal of parenting, and I believe it is, then the best way to instill it is through the demeanor and behavior of a father. Identification with him is a far more efficient teacher than lecturing, scolding, punishing, bribing, and cajoling. Boys watch their dads intently, noting every minor detail of behavior and values. Your sons will imitate much of what you do. If you blow up regularly and insult your wife, drink to excess, curse, smoke, or fight with your coworkers, your boys will probably follow suit. If you are selfish or mean or angry, you'll see those characteristics displayed in the next generation.

Fortunately, the converse is also true. If you are honest, trustworthy, caring, loving, self-disciplined, and God-fearing, your boys will be influenced by those traits as they age. If you are deeply committed to Jesus Christ and live by biblical principles, your children will probably follow in your footsteps.

> Someone said, "I'd rather see a sermon than hear one." There is truth to this statement. Children may not remember what you say, but they are usually impacted for life by what you do. Your son needs to see you doing what is right, even when it is inconvenient to do so.

Traditionally, men have played four roles at home. The first contribution is to serve as the *family provider*—the one responsible to assure that the financial needs of the family are met. The second is to serve as the *loving leader of the clan*, the final arbitrator on issues of substance within the family. The third contribution is to serve as *protector* of each member of the family. And the fourth contribution made by an effective dad is to provide *spiritual direction at home.* It is his responsibility to read the Scriptures to his children and to teach them the fundamentals of their faith. He is the interpreter of the family's moral code and sacred rituals, and he makes sure the children go to church every week.

There is timeless wisdom in these traditional roles. Each of them is rooted in biblical teachings, and men have been defined by these responsibilities for millennia, despite the ridicule some place on them today.

> *I urge you to provide the modeling on which your boys can build their masculine identities. As you carry out the traditional roles we have described, or some version of them, your sons will observe who you are and thereby learn to serve in a similar way when they are grown. That's why any advice to dads about raising boys must begin with an examination of their individual demeanor and character.*

All Boy

We have a nine-year-old boy who is quiet, careful, thoughtful, and very, very shy. Does that mean he is not "all boy"? Should we be trying to change him, to make him more assertive and aggressive?

From a Concerned Parent

The wonderful thing about the way human beings are designed is their marvelous variability and complexity. We are all different and unique. My description of aggressive, risk-taking boys represents an effort to characterize young males, showing what is typical and how they are different from their sisters. However, they also differ from one another on a thousand traits. I remember taking my ten-year-old son and his friend on a skiing trip one day. As we rode the gondola to the top of the mountain, I prepared to take a picture of the two boys with the beautiful landscape visible behind them. Ryan, my son, was smiling and clowning for the camera, while Ricky was just sitting quietly. Ryan then asked Ricky to wave and goof off like he was doing. Ricky replied solemnly, "I'm not that kind of person." It was true. The two boys were at opposite ends of the continuum in their personalities. I still have that picture of the two kids—one going crazy and the other appearing bored half to death. Each of them "all boy."

Your son is certainly not alone in his characteristic shyness. According to the New York Longitudinal Study, approximately 15 percent of babies are somewhat quiet and passive in the nursery.[20] That feature of their temperaments tends to be persistent throughout childhood and beyond. They may be very spontaneous or funny when they are comfortable at home. When they are with strangers, however, their tongues are thrust into their cheeks and they don't know what to say. Some kids are like this because they have been hurt or rejected in the past. The more likely explanation is that they were born that way. Some parents are embarrassed by the introversion of their children and try to change them. It is a fool's errand. No amount of goading or pushing by their parents will make them outgoing, flamboyant, and confident.

My advice to you is to go with the flow.
Accept your child just the way he is made.
Then look for those special qualities
that give your boy individuality and potential.
Nurture him. Cultivate him.
And then give him time to develop
into his own unique personality
like no other human being on earth.

Accept your son

just the way he is made.

Sons and Their Relationships with Girls

Specific life instruction that dads should transmit to their sons could fill many books, but I'll focus on the subtopic of what a father should teach his boys specifically about girls and women. They are unlikely to learn it anywhere else.

I'm going to throw some suggestions at you now in rapid succession, assuming you are a father of one or more boys. Here we go:

> *If you speak disparagingly of the opposite sex,*
> *or if you refer to females as sex objects, those*
> *attitudes will translate directly into your*
> *son's dating and marital relationships later*
> *on. It all starts with your example.*

Remember that your goal is to prepare a boy to lead a family when he's grown and to show him how to earn the respect of those he serves. Tell him it is great to laugh and have fun with his friends, but advise him not to be "goofy." Guys who are goofy are not respected, and people, especially girls and women, do not follow boys and men whom they disrespect.

Also, tell your son that he is never to hit or hurt a girl under any circumstances; rather, he should respect her and protect her if she is threatened. When he is walking with a girl on the street, he should walk on the outside, nearer the cars—symbolic of his responsibility to take care of her. When he is on a date, he should pay for her food and entertainment. Guys must be the initiators, planning the dates and asking for the girl's company. Teach your son to open doors for girls and to help them with their coats or their chairs in a restaurant. When a guy goes to her house to pick up his date, tell him to get out of the car and knock on the door. Never honk. Teach him to stand, in formal situations, when a woman leaves the room or a table or when she returns. This is a way of showing respect for her.

If he treats her like a lady,
she will treat him like a man.
It's a great plan.

Make a concerted effort to teach sexual abstinence to your teenagers, just as you teach them to abstain from drug and alcohol usage and other harmful behavior. Of course you can do it! Young people are fully capable of understanding that irresponsible sex is not in their best interest and that it leads to disease, unwanted pregnancy, rejection, etc. In many cases today, no one is sharing this truth with teenagers. Parents are embarrassed to talk about sex, and, it disturbs me to say, churches are often unwilling to address the issue. Very little support is provided even for young people who are desperately looking for a valid reason to say no. Instead, they're told that "safe sex" is fine if they just use the right equipment.

Your goal is to prepare a boy to lead a family when he's grown.

You as a father must counterbalance those messages at home. Tell your sons that there is no safety—no place to hide—when one lives in contradiction to the laws of God! Remind them repeatedly and emphatically of the biblical teaching about sexual immorality—and why someone who violates those laws not only hurts himself, but also wounds the girl and cheats the man she will eventually marry. Tell them not to take anything that doesn't belong to them, especially the moral purity of a woman. And make it clear that sexual morality is not just right and proper; it is one of the keys to a healthy marriage and family life.

> *Tell your boys that sex is progressive in nature. Kissing and fondling will lead inevitably to greater familiarity. That is just the way we are made. If guys are determined to remain moral, they must take steps to slow down the physical progression early in the relationship.*

> *Tell them not to start the engine if they don't intend to let it run.*

Don't Rush, Don't Cling

Your task is to build a man out of the raw materials
available in your delightful little boy, stone upon
stone upon stone. This task must be your highest
priority for a period of time. It will not always be
required of you. Before you know it, that child at your
feet will become a young man who will pack his bags
and take his first halting steps into the adult world.
Raising children who have been loaned to us for a
brief moment outranks every other responsibility.
Besides, living by that priority when kids are small will
produce the greatest rewards at maturity.

If it seems to you that we are making our kids grow up too fast these days, you are correct. Far too many parents seem to be in a big hurry to make teenagers out of their kids. Some parents arrange actual "dates" for their ten- or twelve-year-olds and give them adult materials to read. You are right to resist this tendency to rush your children through childhood.

Parents in the past had a better understanding of the need for an orderly progression through childhood. Kids in that day were given plenty of time to play and giggle and be themselves. There were cultural "markers" that determined the ages at which certain behaviors were appropriate. Boys, for example, wore short pants until they were twelve or thirteen. Now those markers have disappeared, or they have been moved downward. Children are depicted on TV as having more insight and maturity than their elders. They are rushed, ready or not, from the womb to the nursery school to the adult world at a breakneck pace.

This scurrying to maturity leaves a child without a strong foundation on which to build, because it takes time to build a healthy human being. When you rush the process, your kids have to deal with sexual and peer pressures for which their young minds are not prepared. There is another problem with making children grow up too quickly. When you treat them as though they are adults, it becomes more difficult to set limits on their adolescent behavior down the road. How can you establish a curfew for a thirteen-year-old rebel who has been taught to think of himself as your peer?

Besides, what's the big hurry, anyway?
You are right to savor those childhood years
and let the developmental process march
to its own internal drumbeat.

On the other hand, I get questions from parents about when it is time to let go. For instance, a sixteen-year-old son wants to go on a supervised, three-week outing in a nearby national forest. The boys will eat off the land as much as possible and learn to deal with nature on its own terms. The parents are reluctant to let him go, however. It scares them to think of him being out there somewhere beyond their ability to help him if he gets in difficulty. It just seems safer to keep him at home. Are they right to turn him down?

I remind those parents that within a couple of years, their son will be gone off to college or to some other pursuit, perhaps the military, and he will be entirely beyond their reach. Why not give him a taste of that independence now, while he is still under their care? It will be better for him to ease away from their influence than to have it come to a sudden end.

There was a moment during my teen years when my mother and I had a similar debate. I was sixteen years old

Savor the childhood years and let the developmental process march to its own internal drumbeat.

and had been invited to work on a shrimp boat during the summer. The captain and crew were tough dudes who didn't put up with any nonsense. It was a man's world, and I was drawn to it. My mother was very reluctant to grant permission because she understood that there could be dangers out there in the Gulf of Mexico for four days. She was about to say no when I said, "How long are you going to keep me as your little boy? I'm growing up, and I want to go." With that, she relented. It turned out to be a good experience during which I learned what it is like to work whether or not I felt like it, and I began to understand better how the adult world works. I came back grimy and tired but feeling very good about myself. My mother later acknowledged that she had done the right thing, even though she worried the entire time.

> There's a balance between letting your son grow up according to his own internal drumbeat and easing him away from your influence to walk on his own. "Letting go" works best as a gradual process. It's time to get started.

Winning and Losing

In preparation for the 1914 expedition to the bottom
of the world by the ship Endurance, *Captain Earnest*
Shackleton placed the following ad in local newspapers:
"Men wanted for hazardous duty. Small wages. Bitter
cold. Long months of complete darkness, constant
danger. Safe return doubtful. Honor and recognition
in case of success." More than five thousand men
applied, of which twenty-seven were accepted!
So why were so many men willing to risk everything
to be part of this perilous adventure?
The masculine thirst for conquest.

It is likely that your boy possesses a measure of this competitive and adventuresome spirit. If you understand and respond to this nature, both you and your son will be more in sync. As a place to start, you need to teach him not only how to win but also how to lose gracefully. A good way to do that is by carefully supervising his participation in organized sports, using games as a stimulus for what you want to teach. Coaches and parents must model good sportsmanship, self-control, and teamwork and teach them to their kids. The better athletes among them must not be permitted to taunt the boys who are smaller and less coordinated. Cruelty on the athletic field has no place in the world of the young, although it usually exists there. Finally, adults should resist vigorously the idea of "winning at any cost," which has become so common in children's organized sports. It is shameful the way some parents and coaches act in front of impressionable boys and girls.

Your attitude as a parent will shape the future behavior of your boy. If he sees you yelling at the umpire or referee, taunting other players, and throwing tantrums when things go wrong, he will behave just as badly.

Remember that winning at this age is nothing; teaching your boy to deal properly with his anger, disappointment, and frustration is everything.

This does not mean that you should belittle or ignore his feelings in difficult moments. In fact, you must never underestimate how bad your boy feels when he does poorly at something important to him. The issue is not just that he lost but that he embarrassed himself at having failed. It goes straight to his heart. Let your son talk about the experience and help him understand that there will be wins and losses for the rest of his life. Tell about times when you played well and other days when you flopped. In so doing, you will be modeling how to deal with each outcome. One's successes are not as wonderful as they appear, but neither are the failures as awful as they seem at the time.

There's a lesson here for every parent, too, not only with regard to sports but everything else. Children are going to disappoint us. It's an inevitable part of being young. And when they do, our natural reaction will be to bark at them,

"Why did you do that?" or, "How could you have been so stupid?" But if we're wise, we'll remember that they're just immature little human beings like we used to be.

There are times to say
with love and warmth,
"That's okay, Son. You'll do
better next time."

Boys in School

*Too many boys get off to a bad start in school
and begin feeling "dumb" and inadequate.*

Almost every authority on child development recognizes that schools are typically not set up to accommodate the unique needs of boys. Elementary classrooms, especially, are designed primarily by women to fit the temperament and learning styles of girls. This disadvantage for boys is largely unintentional and is simply the way schools have always functioned. Harvard psychologist and author William S. Pollock said it this way:

"Girls care more about school. They cope with it. Boys don't. Boys are taught at a tempo that doesn't fit them. They are taught in a way that makes them feel inadequate, and if they speak up, they are sent to the principal."[21]

Children are also being placed in formalized educational settings at younger ages, which is very hard on boys. They tend to be six months behind girls in development at six years of age, which makes it tough for many of them to sit quietly and work with pencils and paper and to cope with the social pressures suddenly thrown at them.

Furthermore, schools are too unstructured, if anything, rather than being too rigid. Discipline is what makes learning possible. Thus, I am not critical of schools for requiring order and deportment, but the fact remains that the way boys are constructed makes it harder for them to conform to school, especially when they are young. At least, we as parents should understand what is going on and try to help them fit in. Let's talk about some of those approaches.

First, consider the two kinds of children who are seen commonly in every school classroom. Those in the first category are by nature rather organized individuals who care about details and take their assignments very seriously.

To do poorly on a test depresses them for several days. Parents of these children don't have to monitor their progress to keep them working. It is their way of life.

In the second category are the boys and girls who just don't adapt well to the structure of the classroom. They're sloppy, disorganized, flighty, have a natural aversion to work, and their only great passion is play. These classic underachievers also become impervious to adult pressure. They withstand a storm of parental protest when the report cards come out and then slip back into apathy when no one's looking. They don't even hear the assignments being given in school, and they seem not to be embarrassed in the least when they fail to complete them.

> God made a huge number of these kids, most
> of them boys. They drive their parents to
> distraction, and their unwillingness to work
> can turn their homes into World War III.

If you have one of these flighty boys, it is important to understand that they are not intrinsically inferior to their hardworking siblings. Yes, it would be wonderful if every student used his talent to best advantage, but each child is a unique individual who doesn't have to fit the same mold as everyone else. Besides, the low achiever, such as Albert Einstein, Thomas Alva Edison, Eleanor Roosevelt, Winston Churchill, and many other highly successful people, sometimes outperforms the young superstar in the long run. Never write off that disorganized and apparently lazy kid as a lifelong loser. He or she could surprise you. In the meantime, there are ways that you can help.

One thing is certain: Getting mad at this youngster will not solve the problem. You will never transform an underachieving youngster into a scholar by nagging, pushing, threatening, or punishing. It just isn't in him. If you try to squeeze him into something he's not, you'll only aggravate yourself and wound the child. His disorganization is a product of his laid-back temperament and elements of immaturity— not rebellion or deliberate disobedience. Testosterone is in there working on him too.

You should, on the other hand, stay as close as possible to this child's school. Your boy isn't going to tell you what's going on in the classroom, so you will need to find out for yourself. Seek tutorial assistance, if possible, to help him keep up. Clearly, your child lacks the discipline to structure his life. If he's going to learn it, you will have to teach it to him. Finally, having done what you can to help, accept the best he can give. Go with the flow and begin searching for other areas of success.

The disorganized boy in elementary school is likely to remain flighty as he grows older unless he gets help. That characteristic of his temperament is deeply ingrained and becomes the primary source of his academic problems. It doesn't just "go away" quickly. What can parents do to help? Missing organizational skills in these cases can be learned, and the sooner the better. A good tutor usually knows how to teach them. This early training must be completed before junior high school, where multiple teachers each day will be distributing handouts, assignments, and projects drawn from different textbooks. How are children supposed to know how to handle this requirement of a high level of organization if they have never been taught? Boys also need to learn how to complete long-term assignments little by little. The right supervision can help a flighty adolescent become more self-disciplined and self-propelled in time— even if he never performs quite like the natural scholar.

There is one other factor that must be given the greatest priority. If your son does not learn to read properly, everything else will be in jeopardy. He is also likely to struggle with a damaged self-concept. Almost every youngster can master this skill if approached properly and with methods that suit his learning style. As a place to start, I am among those who believe in teaching phonics, which are still not incorporated in many public-school reading programs. For whatever reasons, millions of kids are illiterate when they graduate from high school. Wonderful opportunities to make readers of them were squandered when they were in elementary school.

> *As a parent, I would turn heaven and earth to find someone who could teach my child to read. There are gifted tutors in almost every community, and there are private organizations that guarantee they can teach your child to read. Even if you have to hock the house to pay for it, I urge you to solve this problem. It is the key to all academic objectives, and a world of adventure awaits those who learn to read.*

If your son does not learn to read properly, everything else will be in jeopardy.

Protecting
Your Family

I will set no wicked thing before mine eyes.

Psalm 101:3, KJV

For Christian parents, the struggle to protect children from the culture goes far beyond junk food and celebrities pushing sneakers. Indeed, today's kids have been bombarded by today's postmodern system with more dangerous ideas than any generation in American history. This system of thought, also called moral relativism, teaches that truth is not only unknowable from God, whom postmodernism perceives as a myth, or from man, who has no right to speak for the rest of us. Rather, truth doesn't exist at all. Nothing is right or wrong, nothing is good or evil, nothing is positive or negative. Everything is relative. All that matters is "what's right for me and what's right for you."

Now what does this moral relativism have to do with raising boys? Just about everything, in fact. It has confused all the age-old distinctions between right and wrong, between proper and improper, between priceless and worthless, and between human and inhuman. Boys, with their tendencies to push the limits and defy authority, are the ones most vulnerable to it. They are enticed into terribly destructive behavior that would have been stopped cold in its tracks by previous generations, who knew that some things are unquestionably wrong and that all ideas have consequences.

> *It has become a daunting task for mothers and fathers to shield them from enticements of every stripe, including those that now inhabit the Internet.*

I hope you will read very carefully what I am about to write now, because it explains why this matter is so significant. Porn and smut pose an awesome threat to your boys. A single exposure to it by some thirteen- to fifteen-year-olds is all that is required to create a full-blown addiction that will hold them in bondage for a lifetime. It is more addictive than cocaine or heroin. That was one of the conclusions drawn during the Attorney General's Commission on Pornography, on which I served. It is a huge cultural problem. More than 40 percent of pastors are afflicted by it![22] How did they get that way? By exposure to graphic materials that set them aflame. This pattern is responsible for untold numbers of divorces and dysfunctional marriages. Availability of the Internet has increased the incidence of this tragedy immeasurably.

I strongly urge you to get television sets, computers, or DVD players out of the bedroom. Locate them in the family room, where they can be monitored and where the amount of time spent on them is regulated. And you must set the filters on their phones and other handheld devices. How can you do less for your children?

It is also our responsibility to watch various forms of entertainment with our boys and girls when they are young. What you see together can present teaching situations that

will help them make the right choices for themselves when they are older. Our children may resist our efforts to screen out the filth and violence that now permeates their world, but they know it's right to do so. They will respect us for saying, "God gave us this home, and we're not going to insult Him by polluting it with foul programming." However, in order to make this judgment, you have to be watching with your children to know what requires your attention. May I suggest that you read and discuss the following verse from the writings of the apostle Paul:

> *Finally, brethren, whatsoever things are true, whatsoever things are honest, whatsoever things are just, whatsoever things are pure, whatsoever things are lovely, whatsoever things are of good report; if there be any virtue, and if there be any praise, think on these things.*

Philippians 4:8, KJV

Your son may resist your efforts to screen out the filth and violence that permeates his world, but he knows it's right to do so.

Disciplining Boys

*What has become of the backbone of parents today?
My husband and I have been amazed again and again
by the fearfulness of parents to take a stand—even with
their small children. They don't seem to grasp the idea
that God has put them in charge for a very good reason,
and it is He who will hold them accountable. If parents
were to instill the concept of proper, God-honoring
authority in their children from the start, it would be far
easier to enforce when the preteen years arrive.*

From a Concerned Mother

It is my opinion that parents today are more confused than ever about effective and loving discipline. It has become a lost art, a forgotten skill. Well-meaning moms and dads have been misled by the liberal tenets of a postmodern culture, especially in regard to its permissiveness as concerns naughty or rebellious behavior. Let me remind you:

> *Self-discipline must be taught. Shaping and molding young minds is a product of careful and diligent parental leadership and requires great effort and patience.*

Boys need structure, they need supervision, and they need to be civilized. When raised in a laissez-faire environment that is devoid of leadership, they often begin to challenge social conventions and common sense. Many often crash and burn during the adolescent years. Some never fully recover. Here's a metaphor that may be helpful: A stream without banks becomes a swamp. It is your job as parents to build the channel in which the stream will run. And another: A child will be ruled by either the rudder or the rock. Authority, when balanced by love, is the rudder that steers your boys around the jagged boulders that could rip the bottom out of their fragile boats. Without you, disaster is inevitable.

Mom and Dad are the authority figures, who must not tolerate rebellious or disrespectful behavior. When your son insists on breaking the rules, he is disciplined just enough to make him uncomfortable. No, you don't chase the youngster away, but you should make it clear that you are unhappy with the way he has behaved. This may be accomplished by a reasonable (but not severe) spanking in instances when the misbehavior has been defiant and disrespectful. Or you could administer a time-out period or other lesser punishment. Whatever the approach, your son must find it unpleasant and aversive.

After the discomfort of that confrontation, there will come a moment when he will ask, symbolically if not in words, "Can I come back again?" At that point, welcome him with open arms. That is the time to explain why he got in trouble and how he can avoid the conflict next time. Never during this process should you resort to screaming or other indications that you are frustrated and out of control; instead, demonstrate mastery of the situation. A few quiet words spoken with conviction by a mother or father can often convey this confidence and authority better than a barrage of empty threats and wild gestures.

Many parents today are afraid to show displeasure to kids for fear of wounding or rejecting them. To the contrary, little people need to know who is in charge and that they are "safe" in that person's care. Reminding a child that you are a benevolent boss emphasizes that you expect to be obeyed.

There are times when you need to get down on one knee, look your boy straight in the eye, and say confidently but without anger, "I don't want you to misbehave again. Is that clear?" Without screaming or threatening, your tone of voice says, "Take seriously what I'm saying."

It takes a great deal of patience and sensitivity to discern how your son is responding. If you listen carefully, he will tell you what he's thinking and feeling. There's a time for affirmation, tenderness, and love. They nourish the spirit and seal the bond between generations.

But there's also a time for discipline and punishment. Moms and dads who try to be eternally positive, ignoring irresponsibility or defiance in their children, fail to teach them that behavior has consequences. But beware! Parents who are continually punitive and accusatory can create serious behavioral and emotional problems. The apostle Paul recognized this danger and cautioned dads not to get carried away with discipline. He said, "Fathers, do not exasperate your children; instead, bring them up in the training and instruction of the Lord" (Ephesians 6:4). He mentioned the warning again in Colossians 3:21: "Fathers, do not embitter your children, or they will become discouraged." Remember that Paul also said emphatically to children, "Obey your parents in everything, for this pleases the Lord" (Colossians 3:20). What great wisdom there is in those convergent passages.

> *Balance in discipline holds the key to the entire parent-child relationship. None of us does it perfectly. But the best parents are those who steer a path between permissiveness and authoritarianism. Your boys, especially, will thrive under your leadership if you avoid the extremes and are careful to "season" your relationship with love.*

The Priority
of Time and Faith

So many of the difficulties that confront our kids

come down to a single characteristic of today's families:

There is nobody home.

We have considered the burgeoning crisis that confronts our boys in today's cultural context. Working against them are the breakup of families, the absence or disengagement of dads, the consequent wounding of spirits, and the postmodern culture that is twisting and warping so many of our children. If there is a common theme that connects each of these sources of difficulty, it is the frantic pace of living that has left too little time or energy for the children who look to us for the fulfillment of every need, leading to the increasing isolation and detachment it produces.

America's love affair with materialism has taken its toll on the things that matter most. As a case in point, consider the epidemic of bullying and taunting that is occurring in our schools. All of us experienced similar difficult moments when we were young. So what is different now? It is the absence of parents, who have nothing left to give. Some of us as kids came home to intact and caring families that were able to "talk us down" from the precipice, to assure us of their love, and to help us see that the harsh judgment of our peers was not the end of the world. In the absence of that kind of wise counsel in times of crisis, today's kids have nowhere to go with their rage. Some resort to drugs or alcohol, some withdraw into isolation, and some, sadly, vent their anger in murderous assault. If only Mom and Dad had been there when the passions peaked.

As we have seen repeatedly in these chapters, it is boys who typically suffer most from the absence of parental care. It is my conviction that those who choose to bring a child into the world must give that boy or girl highest priority for a period of time. In a very short time, they will be grown up and on their own.

However, it is not enough simply to be at home and available to our children. We must use the opportunities of these few short years to teach them our values and beliefs. Millions of young people who have grown up in the relative opulence of North America have not had that training. They are terribly confused about transcendent values.

> *We have given them more material*
> *blessings than any generation in history.*
> *More money has been spent on their*
> *education, medical care, entertainment,*
> *and travel than any who have gone before.*
> *Yet we have failed them in the most*
> *important of all parental responsibilities:*
>
> *We have not taught them who they are as*
> *children of God or what they have been*
> *placed here to do.*

Human beings tend to struggle with troubling questions they can't answer. Just as nature abhors a vacuum, so the intellect acts to fill the void. Or to state it differently, it seeks to repair a hole in its system of beliefs. That is why so many young people today chase after twisted and alien "theologies," such as New Age nonsense, the pursuit of pleasure, substance abuse, and illicit sex. They are searching vainly for something that will satisfy their "soul hunger," but are unlikely to find it. Not even great achievement and superior education will put the pieces together.

> *Meaning in life comes only by answering eternal questions such as "Who am I?" "How did I get here?" and "Is there life after death?" They are adequately addressed only in the Christian faith. No other religion can tell us who we are, how we got here, and where we are going after death. And no other belief system teaches that we are known and loved individually by the God of the universe and by His only Son, Jesus Christ.*

These commandments that I give you today are to be upon your hearts. Impress them on your children. Talk about them when you sit at home and when you walk along the road, when you lie down and when you get up. Tie them as symbols on your hands and bind them on your foreheads. Write them on the doorframes of your houses and on your gates.

Deuteronomy 6:6-9

Your Number One Task

At the top of the list of what children need from parents during the developmental years is an understanding of who God is and what He expects them to do. This teaching must begin very early in childhood. Even at three years of age, a child is capable of learning that the flowers, the sky, the birds, and even the rainbow are gifts from God's hand. He made these wonderful things, just as He created each one of us. The first Scripture our children should learn is, "God is love" (1 John 4:8). They should be taught to thank Him before eating their food and to ask for His help when they are hurt or scared.

Moses takes that responsibility a step further in Deuteronomy 6. He tells parents to talk about spiritual matters continually. If this passage means anything, it is that we are to give the greatest emphasis to the spiritual development of our children. Nothing even comes close to it in significance. The only way you can be with your precious children in the next life is to introduce them to Jesus Christ and His teachings, hopefully when they are young and impressionable. This is Task Number One in child-rearing.

Not only is spiritual development of relevance to eternity, it is also critical to the way your children will live out their days on this earth. Specifically, boys need to be well established in their faith in order to understand the meaning of good and evil. They are growing up in a postmodern world in which all ideas are considered equally valid and nothing is really wrong. Wickedness is bad only in the minds of those who think it is bad. People who live by this godless outlook on life are headed for great pain.

The Christian worldview, by contrast, teaches that good and evil are determined by the God of the universe and that He has given us an unchanging moral standard by which to live. He also offers forgiveness from sins,

which boys (and girls) have good reason to need. Only with this understanding is a child being prepared to face the challenges that lie ahead. Yet most American children receive no spiritual training whatsoever! They are left to make it up as they go along, which leads to the meaningless existence we have discussed.

The most effective teaching tool of values and beliefs is in the modeling provided by parents at home.

Children are amazingly perceptive of the things they witness in their parents' unguarded moments. It is one reason why moms and dads must live a morally consistent life in front of their kids. If they hope to win them for Christ, they can't afford to be casual or whimsical about the things they believe. If you act as though there is no absolute truth, and if you are too busy to pray and attend church services together, and if your kids are allowed to play soccer or Little League during Sunday school, and if you cheat on your income tax or lie to the bill collector or fight with your neighbors, your children will get the message. "Dad talks a good game, but he doesn't really believe it." If you serve them this weak soup throughout childhood, they will spew it out when given the opportunity. Any ethical weak spot of this nature—any lack of clarity on matters of right and wrong—will be noted and magnified by the next generation.

> *If you think that faith and belief are routinely absorbed by children, just look at the sons of the great patriarchs of the Bible, from Isaac to Samuel to David to Hezekiah. All of them saw their offspring fall away from the faith of their fathers as the years unfolded.*

The Earlier
the Better

"The earlier the better" when it comes to introducing our children to the Lord. Based on a nationwide representative sampling of more than 4,200 young people and adults, the survey data show that people from ages five through thirteen have a 32 percent probability of accepting Christ as their Savior. Young people from the ages of fourteen through eighteen have just a 4 percent likelihood of doing so, while adults (over nineteen) have only a 6 percent probability of making that choice. The years prior to age twelve are when a majority of children make their decision as to whether or not they will follow Christ.[23]

Furthermore, everything we do during those foundational child-rearing years should be bathed in prayer. There is not enough knowledge in the books—not in this one or any other—to secure the outcome of our parenting responsibility without divine help. It is arrogant to think that we can shepherd our kids safely through the minefields of an increasingly sinful society. That awesome realization hit me when our daughter, Danae, was only three years old. I recognized that having a Ph.D. in child development was not going to be enough to meet the challenges of parenthood. That is why Shirley and I began fasting and praying for Danae, and later for Ryan, almost every week from the time they were young. At least one of us bore that responsibility throughout their childhoods. In fact, Shirley continues that practice to this day. Our petition was the same through the early years:

> "Lord, give us the wisdom to raise the precious children whom you have loaned to us, and above all else, help us bring them to the feet of Jesus. This is more important to us than our health or our work or our finances. What we ask most fervently is that the circle be unbroken when we meet in heaven."

With that, I hasten to a closing thought. Once your children have reached the latter years of adolescence, it will be important not to push them too hard spiritually. You can still have reasonable expectations for them as long as they are under your roof, but you can't demand that they believe what they have been taught. The door must be opened fully to the world outside. This can be the most frightening time of parenthood. The tendency is to retain control in order to keep your kids from making mistakes. However, teenagers and young adults are more likely to make the proper choices when they aren't forced to rebel in order to escape. The simple truth is that love demands freedom. They go hand in hand.

My prayers will be with you as you discharge your God-given responsibility. It's a tall order but one that can be achieved with wisdom

*and guidance from the Father. The primary
mechanism by which these goals are realized
is the application of confident leadership and
discipline at home, tempered with love and
compassion. It is an unbeatable combination.*

*Cherish every moment of it.
And hug your kids while you can.*

"Lord, give us the wisdom to raise the precious son whom you have loaned to us, and above all else, help us bring him to the feet of Jesus."

If you enjoyed *Dads & Sons*, don't miss the
bestseller *Bringing Up Boys*!

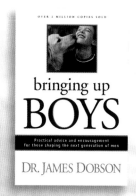
And be sure to tune in to *Dr. James Dobson's Family Talk*.
To learn more or to find a station in your area,
visit www.drjamesdobson.org or call (877) 732-6825.

Endnotes

1   John Rosemond, as quoted in Paula Gray Hunker, "What Are Boys Made Of?" *Washington Times*, September 28, 1999, 1(E).

2   Ibid.

3   Plato, *Laws*, 1953 edition 1, 164.

4   Ira Dreyfuss, "Boys and Girls See Risk Differently, Study Says," Associated Press, February 16, 1997.

5   Robert Sapolsky, "Testosterone Rules: It Takes More Than Just a Hormone to Make a Fellow's Trigger Finger Itch," *Discover*, March 1997, 44.

6   Michael Gurian and Kathy Stevens, *The Minds of Boys* (San Francisco: Jossey-Bass, 2005), 140.

7   Ron G. Rosenfeld and Barbara C. Nicodemus, "The Transition from Adolescence to Adult Life: Physiology of the 'Transition' Phase and Its Evolutionary Basis," *Hormone Research* 60 (2003): 74–77.

8   Joshua Freedman, "Hijacking of the Amygdala," *EQ Today*, April 21, 1999.

9   Hunker, "What Are Boys Made Of?"

10 John Attarian, "Let Boys Be Boys—Exploding Feminist Dogma, This Provocative Book Reveals How Educators Are Trying to Feminize Boys While Neglecting Their Academic and Moral Instruction," *The World and I*, 15 no. 10 (October 2000).

11 See for example: Mary Brown Parlee, "The Sexes under Scrutiny: From Old Biases to New Theories," *Psychology Today* (November 1978): 62-69; Jane O'Reilly, "Doing Away with Sex Stereotypes," *Time*, October 23, 1980, 1.

12 Marlo Thomas et al., *Free to Be You and Me* (Philadelphia: Running Press, 1974).

13 Germaine Greer, *The Female Eunuch* (London: MacGibbon and Kee, 1970).

14 "No Safe Place: Violence against Women: An Interview with Gloria Steinem," KUED-TV, Salt Lake City. Originally found at http://www.media. utah.edu/prdction/interv/steinem.html.

15 Ibid.

16 Elisabeth Bumiller, "Gloria Steinem: The Everyday Rebel; Two Decades of Feminism, and the Fire Burns as Bright," *Washington Post*, October 12, 1983, 1(B).

17 Ibid.

18 Greer, *The Female Eunuch*.